Collins
First
Spanish
Picture
Dictionary

Written by Irene Yates
Illustrated by Nick Sharratt
Consultant Editor: Ginny Lapage

Collins

Art Director: Rachel Hamdi
Design Consultant: Sophie Stericker
Cover Designer: Nicola Croft
Designers: Holly Mann, Sarah Borny
Translation: Lifeline Language Services Ltd.

First published in 2005 by Collins

© HarperCollins*Publishers* Ltd 2005

Published by Collins
a division of HarperCollins*Publishers* Ltd
77-85 Fulham Palace Road, London W6 8JB

www.collins.co.uk

Browse the complete Collins Education catalogue at:
www.collinseducation.com

ISBN 978 0 00 720347 5

10 9

Printed in China

Contents

How to use this book

Children love playing with words, and learning a new language can be lots of fun. This colourful dictionary is specially designed to help you introduce your child to Spanish. With your help, your child will learn key words from a range of familiar situations, discovering new sounds along the way. They will also start to recognize some of the differences and similarities between Spanish and English.

First steps to learning Spanish

As soon as they are comfortable expressing themselves in their own language, children are ready to learn a new one. To get the best out of this book, sit with your child and encourage them to look at the pictures, to say the Spanish words as often as possible,

Tom

Elisha

Jake

Read the heading out loud so your child knows the context of the Spanish words.

Point to the picture, then run your finger along the Spanish words, from left to right, saying the words out loud. Ask you child to repeat the words, not forgetting to say the short word in front.

Compare the Spanish word with the English, pointing out the similarities as well as the differences between the two languages.

Look for me on every page – sometimes you will have to look very hard! It's fun to see what I'm doing.

Having fun at playschool

el ordenador
computer

la maestra
teacher

el libro
book

las tijeras
scissors

las acuarelas
paint

el pincel
paintbrush

los lápices de colores

el pegamento
glue

12

and to answer all the questions. Come back to the book time and time again, so your child absorbs the new sounds and learns to associate the Spanish words with the pictures.

Questions and answers

Nick Sharratt's lively scenes will help your child to memorize the Spanish words by putting them into context. They also offer plenty of scope for further questions, so you can encourage your child to practice speaking their newly learned words. For your own guidance, there is a pronunciation guide at the back of the book.

Ask the questions, encouraging your child always to answer in Spanish. (The answers will be words featured on the spread.)

Encourage your child to point out and name real objects around them whenever possible.

Make up your own questions, based on what's going on in the picture. Once your child has learned about colours and numbers (see pages 40-43), you can incorporate these in your questions too, for example, "How many paintbrushes can you count?"

Learning the names of the characters will add to the fun your child gets from using this book.

Ask your child to match objects in the main picture with those shown on the left, and vice versa. When looking for an object, encourage your child always to use its Spanish name.

Lucy

Taz

Amy

Fun and games at home

la puerta
door

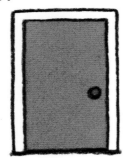

la ventana
window

el sillón
chair

el sofá
sofa

el cojín
cushion

el reloj
clock

el televisor
television

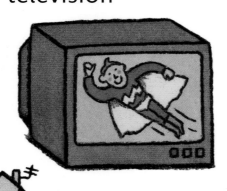

el teléfono
telephone

la cabeza
head

el pelo
hair

la cara
face

la nariz
nose

los ojos
eyes

las orejas
ears

los dientes
teeth

la boca
mouth

el cuello
neck

el hombro
shoulder

What do you smell things with?

Come to my birthday party

el globo
balloon

el antifaz
mask

el regalo
present

la corona
party hat

el helado
ice cream

el pastel
cake

el zumo de frutas
fruit juice

los caramelos
sweets

Having fun at playschool

el ordenador
computer

la maestra
teacher

el libro
book

las tijeras
scissors

las acuarelas
paint

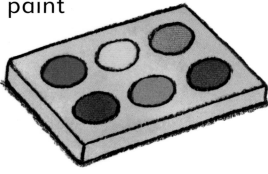

el pincel
paintbrush

los lápices de colores
crayons

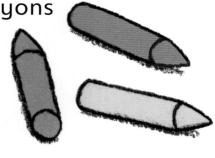

el pegamento
glue

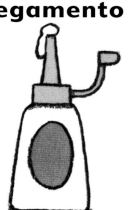

What do we like to wear?

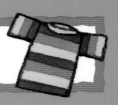

la camisa
shirt

la chaqueta
jacket

el vestido
dress

los pantalones
trousers

la falda
skirt

los pantalones cortos
shorts

los calcetines
socks

los zapatos
shoes

What do you like to wear best?

el pijama
pyjamas

el camisón
nightie

los calzoncillos
pants

las braguitas
knickers

el jersey
jumper

la camiseta
T-shirt

el gorro
hat

los guantes
gloves

15

el cortacésped
lawnmower

la carretilla
wheelbarrow

la mariposa
butterfly

el pájaro
bird

la regadera
watering can

la bicicleta
bike

la piscina
paddling pool

la flor
flower

la casa
house

la tienda
shop

el policía
policeman

la carretera
road

el coche
car

la farola
street light

la silla de ruedas
wheelchair

el semáforo
traffic light

Where do you go to buy things?

Things that go

los patines
rollerblades

el camión
lorry

la moto
motorbike

el autobús
bus

la excavadora
digger

el camión volquete
dumper truck

el barco
boat

el monopatín
skateboard

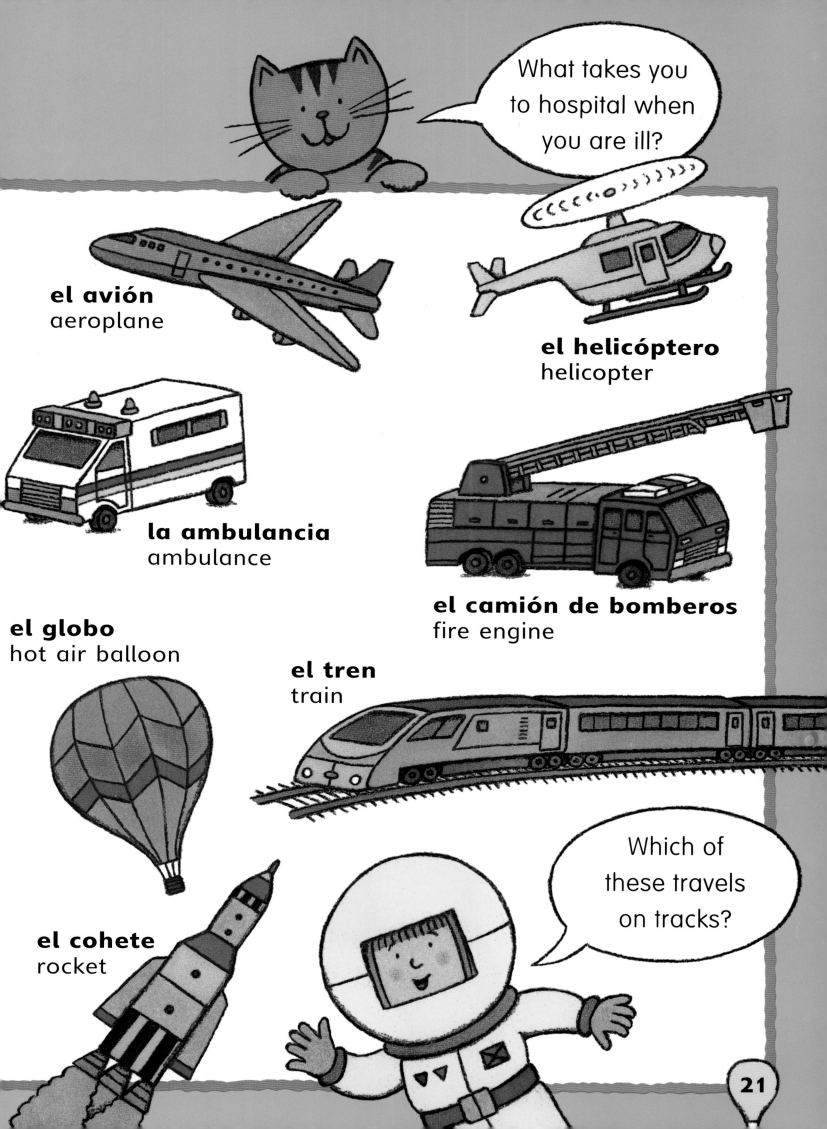

Let's go to the toy shop

el puzzle
jigsaw puzzle

el camión
truck

el garaje
garage

la casita de muñecas
doll's house

el osito de peluche
teddy bear

la muñeca
doll

la marioneta
puppet

los cubos
blocks

At the supermarket

el tarro
jar

la bolsa
bag

el bote
tin

la cesta
basket

el carro
trolley

el dinero
money

la caja
checkout

la botella
bottle

24

Food to help me grow

la fruta
fruit

la verdura
vegetables

el arroz
rice

la hamburguesa
hamburger

**las patatas
fritas**
chips

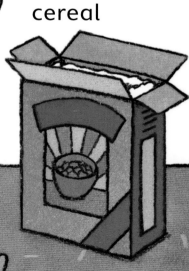

los espaguetis
spaghetti

los cereales
cereal

What do you
eat for breakfast?

Take me to the pet shop

el conejo
rabbit

el hámster
hamster

el gatito
kitten

el perrito
puppy

el pececito
goldfish

la cesta
basket

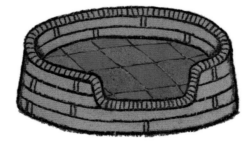

la jaula
cage

el periquito
budgie

What's in the park?

el tobogán
slide

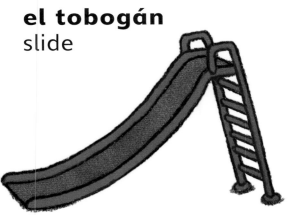

el columpio
swing

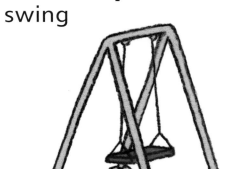

el cochecito
buggy

las barras trepadoras
climbing frame

el banco
bench

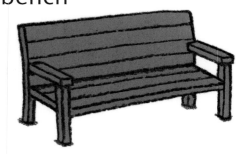

el árbol
tree

el perro
dog

el pato
duck

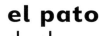

Big beasts and minibeasts

el canguro
kangaroo

la jirafa
giraffe

el león
lion

el oso panda
panda

el elefante
elephant

el cocodrilo
crocodile

la ballena
whale

Down on the farm

el granjero
farmer

el tractor
tractor

la gallina
hen

el cordero
lamb

el caballo
horse

la vaca
cow

la verja
gate

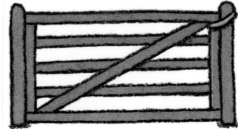

la paja
hay

34

la concha
shell

el cangrejo
crab

la gaviota
seagull

el castillo de arena
sand castle

la pelota
beach ball

la ola
wave

el cubo
bucket

la pala
spade

See what we can do!

él salta
he jumps

él camina
he walks

ella corre
she runs

ella aplaude
she claps

ella lleva
she carries

What is the girl
with the box
doing?

él pinta
he paints

ellos bailan they dance

What is the unhappy boy doing?

él canta
he sings

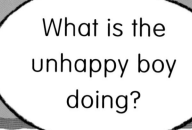

él ríe
he laughs

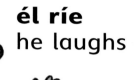

ella se peina
she brushes

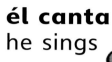

ella corta
she cuts

él llora
he cries

ella come
she eats

ella bebe
she drinks

39

Colours are everywhere

violeta
purple

rojo
red

negro
black

azul
blue

amarillo
yellow

What colour is the bouncy castle?

40

1 uno

How many windows does this house have?

2 dos

3 tres

4 cuatro

5 cinco

Count the spots on the ladybird.

6 seis

7 siete

8 ocho

9 nueve

10 diez

lunes
Monday

martes
Tuesday

miércoles
Wednesday

jueves
Thursday

viernes
Friday

sábado
Saturday

domingo
Sunday

el día
day

la noche
night

What day of the week is it?

What makes you put up your umbrella?

el sol
sun

la lluvia
rain

el viento
wind

la nieve
snow

How the words sound

A

aeroplane	el avión – *el avi-**yo**n*
ambulance	la ambulancia – *la amboo**la**ntheea*
arm	el brazo – *el br**a**tho*

B

bag	la bolsa – *la b**o**lsa*
balloon	el globo – *el gl**o**bo*
basket	la cesta – *la th**e**sta*
beach ball	la pelota – *la pel**o**ta*
bee	la abeja – *la ab**e**kha*
beetle	el escarabajo – *el escarab**a**kho*
bench	el banco – *el b**a**nko*
bike	la bicicleta – *la beethe**e**cleta*
bird	el pájaro – *el p**a**kharo*
biscuits	las galletas – *las gal-**ye**tass*
black	negro – *n**e**gro*
blocks	los cubos – *los k**oo**boss*
blue	azul – *ath**oo**l*
boat	el barco – *el b**a**rko*
book	el libro – *el l**ee**bro*
bottle	la botella – *la bot**e**lya*
bottom	el trasero – *el tr**a**ssero*
bread	el pan – *el pan*

brown	marrón – *mar-r**o**n*
brushes, she	ella se peina – *el-ya se p**ey**na*
bucket	el cubo – *el k**oo**bo*
budgie	el periquito – *el pereek**ee**to*
buggy	el cochecito – *el kochayth**ee**to*
bus	el autobús – *el owtob**oo**ss*
butterfly	la mariposa – *la mareep**o**ssa*

C

cage	la jaula – *la kh**ow**la*
cake	el pastel – *el past**e**l*
car	el coche – *el k**o**chay*
carries, she	ella lleva – *el-ya ly**e**va*
caterpillar	la oruga – *la or**oo**ga*
cereal	los cereales – *los thereya**le**ss*
chair	el sillón – *el seely**o**n*
checkout	la caja – *la k**a**kha*
cheese	el queso – *el k**ay**so*
chicken	el pollo – *el p**o**l-yo*
chips	las patatas fritas – *las pat**a**tas fr**ee**tass*
claps, she	ella aplaude – *el-ya apl**ow**day*
climbing frame	las barras trepadoras – *las b**a**rrass trepad**o**rass*
clock	el reloj – *el ray**lo**kh*
computer	el ordenador – *el ordayn**a**dor*
cow	la vaca – *la b**a**ka*
crab	el cangrejo – *el kangr**e**kho*
crayons	los lápices de colores - *los lap**ee**thess day col**o**ress*
cries, he	él llora – *el l-y**o**ra*
crocodile	el cocodrilo – *el kokodr**ee**lo*
cushion	el cojín – *el kokh**ee**n*
cuts, she	ella corta – *el-ya k**o**rta*

D

dance, they	ellos bailan – *el-yos b**y**-lan*
day	el día – *el d**ee**ya*
digger	la excavadora – *la exkavad**o**ra*
dog	el perro – *el p**e**r-ro*
doll	la muñeca – *la moony**ay**ka*
dolls house	la casita de muñecas – *la kass**ee**ta day moony**ay**kass*
door	la puerta – *la pw**e**rta*